A **Literature Kit**™ FOR

Maniac Magee

By Jerry Spinelli

Written by Eleanor M. Summers

GRADES 5 - 6

Classroom Complete Press
P.O. Box 19729
San Diego, CA 92159
Tel: 1-800-663-3609 | Fax: 1-800-663-3608
Email: service@classroomcompletepress.com

www.classroomcompletepress.com

ISBN – 13: 978-1-55319-242-9
 We acknowledge the financial support of the Government of Canada through the Book Publishing Industry Development Program (BPIDP) for our publishing activities.

Critical Thinking Skills

Maniac Magee

Level	Skills for Critical Thinking	1-5	6-10	11-14	15-21	22-25	26-32	33-35	36-39	40-43	44-46	Writing Tasks	Graphic Organizers
		Chapter Questions											
LEVEL 1 Remembering	• Identify Story Elements	✓	✓	✓	✓	✓	✓	✓	✓	✓	✓	✓	✓
	• Recall Details	✓	✓	✓	✓	✓	✓	✓	✓	✓	✓	✓	✓
	• Match	✓	✓	✓	✓	✓	✓	✓	✓	✓	✓		✓
	• Sequence Events	✓			✓		✓				✓	✓	
LEVEL 2 Understanding	• Compare & Contrast			✓	✓		✓					✓	✓
	• Summarize		✓	✓	✓	✓	✓	✓	✓	✓	✓	✓	✓
	• State Main Idea	✓	✓	✓	✓	✓	✓	✓	✓	✓	✓	✓	✓
	• Describe	✓	✓	✓	✓	✓	✓	✓	✓	✓	✓	✓	✓
	• Explain	✓	✓		✓	✓		✓	✓	✓		✓	✓
LEVEL 3 Applying	• Plan	✓	✓	✓	✓	✓	✓	✓	✓	✓	✓	✓	✓
	• Interview	✓	✓	✓	✓	✓	✓	✓	✓	✓	✓	✓	✓
	• Infer Outcomes		✓	✓	✓	✓	✓	✓	✓	✓	✓	✓	✓
LEVEL 4 Analysing	• Draw Conclusions	✓	✓	✓	✓	✓	✓	✓	✓	✓	✓	✓	✓
	• Identify Supporting Evidence	✓	✓	✓	✓	✓	✓	✓	✓	✓	✓	✓	✓
	• Motivations	✓	✓	✓	✓	✓	✓	✓	✓	✓	✓	✓	✓
	• Identify Cause & Effect	✓		✓	✓			✓			✓	✓	✓
LEVEL 5 Evaluating	• State & Defend An Opinion	✓	✓	✓	✓	✓	✓	✓	✓	✓	✓	✓	✓
	• Make Judgements	✓	✓	✓	✓	✓	✓	✓	✓	✓	✓	✓	✓
LEVEL 6 Creating	• Predict	✓	✓	✓	✓	✓	✓	✓	✓	✓	✓	✓	
	• Design		✓		✓					✓	✓	✓	✓
	• Create		✓		✓					✓	✓	✓	✓
	• Imagine Alternatives	✓			✓	✓	✓	✓	✓	✓	✓	✓	

Based on Bloom's Taxonomy

Contents

✔ **6 BONUS Activity Pages!** **Additional worksheets for your students**

FREE!

Download a digital copy for use with your projection system or interactive whiteboard

Go to our website: **www.classroomcompletepress.com/bonus**

- Enter item CC2527
- Enter pass code CC2527D for Activity Pages

Assessment Rubric

Maniac Magee

Student's Name: ______________ Assignment: ______________ Level: ______

	Level 1	Level 2	Level 3	Level 4
Comprehension of Novel	Demonstrates a limited understanding of the novel	Demonstrates a basic understanding of the novel	Demonstrates a good understanding of the novel	Demonstrates a thorough understanding of the novel
Content • information and details relevant to focus	Elements incomplete; key details missing	Some elements complete; details missing	All required elements completed; key details contain some description	All required elements completed; enough description for clarity
Style • effective word choice and originality • precise language	Little variety in word choice. Language vague and imprecise	Some variety in word choice. Language somewhat vague and imprecise	Good variety in word choice. Language precise and quite descriptive	Writer's voice is apparent throughout. Excellent choice of words. Precise language
Conventions • spelling, language, capitalization, punctuation	Errors seriously interfere with the writer's purpose	Repeated errors in mechanics and usage	Some errors in convention	Few errors in convention

STRENGTHS:

WEAKNESSES:

NEXT STEPS:

Teacher Guide

Our resource has been created for ease of use by both TEACHERS and STUDENTS alike.

Introduction

Our literature kit is designed to give the teacher a number of helpful ways of making the study of this novel a more enjoyable and profitable experience for the students. Our guide features a number of useful and flexible components, from which the teacher can choose. It is not expected that all of the activities will be completed.

One advantage to this approach to the study of a novel is that the student can work at his or her own speed, and the teacher can assign activities that match the student's abilities.

Our literature kit divides the novel by chapters and features reading comprehension and vocabulary questions. Themes include self reliance, adapting to one's environment, relationships with other families, testing and proving oneself, and friendships that crosses barriers. Maniac Magee *provides a wealth of opportunity for classroom discussion because of its vivid portrayal of the central character, and his quest to find his place in the world.*

How Is Our Literature Kit™ Organized?

STUDENT HANDOUTS

Chapter Activities *(in the form of reproducible worksheets)* make up the majority of this resource. For each group of chapters, there are BEFORE YOU READ activities and AFTER YOU READ activities.

- The BEFORE YOU READ activities prepare students for reading by setting a purpose for reading. They stimulate background knowledge and experience, and guide students to make connections between what they know and what they will learn. Important concepts and vocabulary from the chapter(s) are also presented.
- The AFTER YOU READ activities check students' comprehension and extend their learning. Students are asked to give thoughtful consideration of the text through creative and evaluative short-answer questions and journal prompts.

Six **Writing Tasks** and three **Graphic Organizers** are included to further develop students' critical thinking and writing skills, and analysis of the text. *(See page 6 for suggestions on using the Graphic Organizers.)* The **Assessment Rubric** *(page 4)* is a useful tool for evaluating students' responses to the Writing Tasks and Graphic Organizers.

PICTURE CUES

This resource contains three main types of pages, each with a different purpose and use. A **Picture Cue** at the top of each page shows, at a glance, what the page is for.

Teacher Guide
- Information and tools for the teacher

Student Handout
- Reproducible worksheets and activities

Easy Marking™ Answer Key
- Answers for student activities

EASY MARKING™ ANSWER KEY

Marking students' worksheets is fast and easy with this **Answer Key**. Answers are listed in columns—just line up the column with its corresponding worksheet, as shown, and see how every question matches up with its answer!

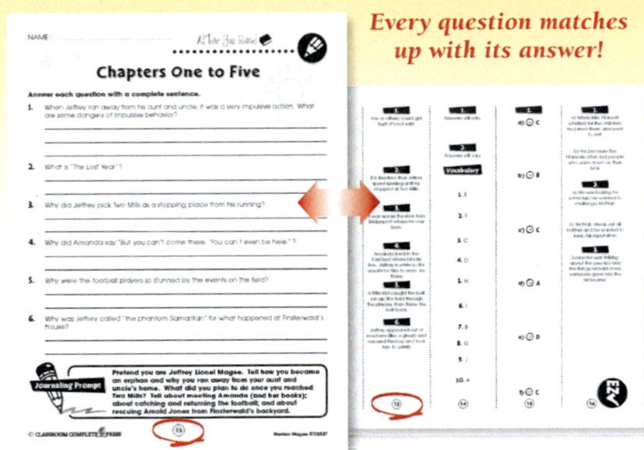

1,2,3
Graphic Organizers

The three **Graphic Organizers** included in this **Literature Kit™** are especially suited to a study of ***Maniac Magee***. Below are suggestions for using each organizer in your classroom, or they may also be adapted to suit the individual needs of your students. The organizers can be used on a projection system or interactive whiteboard in teacher-led activities, small group activities, and/or photocopied for use as student worksheets. To evaluate students' responses to any of the organizers,you may wish to use the **Assessment Rubric** *(on page 4)*.

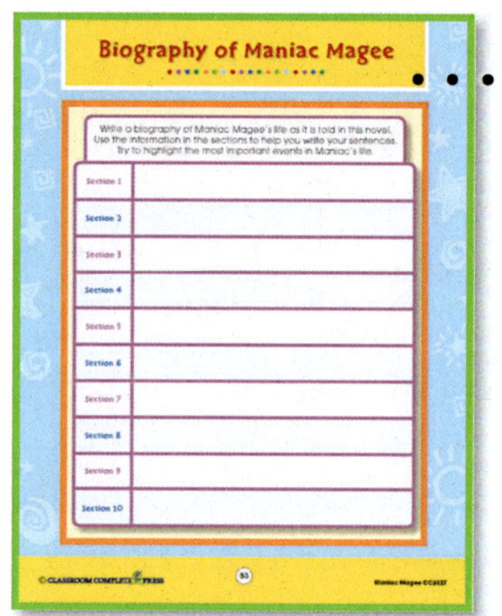

BIOGRAPHY OF MANIAC MAGEE

This activity is a culminating activity resulting from classroom discussion and questioning inherent in the study of such a novel. The teacher may choose to do this summary with a small group of students who are ready for this activity, or as a whole group with strong direction from the teacher. Students are required to identify such critical concepts as setting, protagonist/antagonist (if it applies), conflict, climax, falling action, point of view, theme, and conclusion. It is meant to serve as an effective wrap-up in such a novel study. Found on Page 53.

NEW TV SHOW

The student has the opportunity to use their knowledge of television miniseries shows to create the introductory show for *Maniac Magee*. It would be helpful to discuss the features required to make an interesting first show and to list those features for student referral. An extended activity might be to have a group of students dramatize the introductory show.
Found on Page 54.

NOW THAT'S FUNNY!

Maniac Magee is an incredible novel dealing with themes of survival, isolation, racial issues, and finding one's place in the world. It tells the story of a young boy searching for a home and someone to love him. The author does this with quick sayings and humorous situations. *In Now That's Funny!*, students are asked to describe and illustrate a humorous situation using a comic book format. Found on Page 55.

Bloom's Taxonomy* for Reading Comprehension

The activities in this resource engage and build the full range of thinking skills that are essential for students' reading comprehension. Based on the six levels of thinking in Bloom's Taxonomy, questions are given that challenge students to not only recall what they have read, but to move beyond this to understand the text through higher-order thinking. By using higher-order skills of applying, analyzing, evaluating and creating, students become active readers, drawing more meaning from the text, and applying and extending their learning in more sophisticated ways.

This **Literature Kit™**, therefore, is an effective tool for any Language Arts program. Whether it is used in whole or in part, or adapted to meet individual student needs, this resource provides teachers with the important questions to ask, inspiring students' interest and creativity, and promoting meaningful learning.

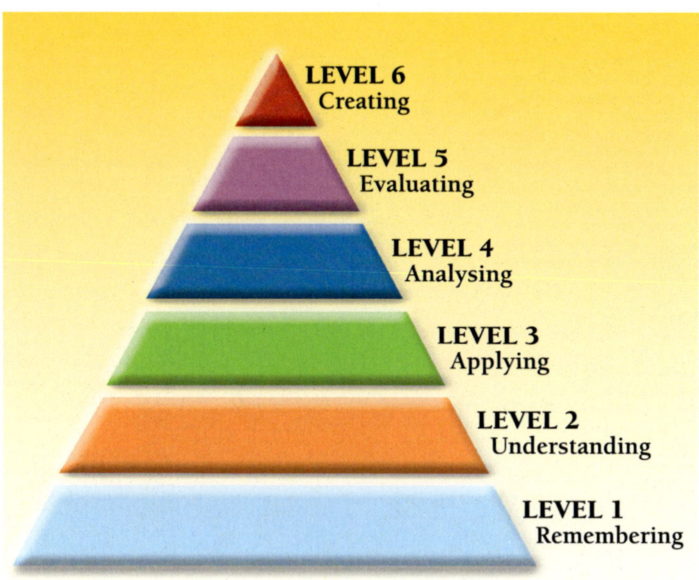

BLOOM'S TAXONOMY: 6 LEVELS OF THINKING

**Bloom's Taxonomy is a widely used tool by educators for classifying learning objectives, and is based on the work of Benjamin Bloom.*

Teaching Strategies

WHOLE-CLASS, SMALL GROUP AND INDEPENDENT STUDY

This study guide contains the following activities:

Before Reading Activities: themes are introduced and thought-provoking questions put forward for the students to consider.

Vocabulary Activities: new and unfamiliar words are introduced and reviewed.

After Reading Questions: the first part of this section includes short answer questions dealing with the content of the text. The second part features questions that are more open-ended and feature concepts from the higher order of Bloom's Taxonomy.

Writing Tasks: creative writing assignments based on Bloom's Taxonomy that relate to the plot of the particular chapters.

A comprehension quiz is also included comprised of multiple-choice, true/false and short-answer questions.

Graphic Organizers: three full-page reproducible sheets have been included and can be used for teaching purposes throughout the text.

Bonus Sheets are also available online.

The study guide can be used in a variety of ways in the classroom depending on the needs of the students and teacher. The teacher may choose to use an independent reading approach with students capable of working independently. It also works well with small groups, with most of the lessons being quite easy to follow. Finally, in other situations, teachers will choose to use it with their entire class.

Teachers may wish to have their students keep a daily reading log so that they might record their daily progress and reflections.

Summary of the Story

Maniac Magee *is a humorous story of a young boy out to survive on his own terms. Jeffrey Lionel Magee is a normal boy who is suddenly made an orphan by a tragic accident. He is sent to live with his very rigid aunt and uncle who really don't want him but are following a sense of duty to raise him. Finally, he cannot endure any longer and decides to run away. But he does more than just run away, he becomes an outstanding runner. He engages in a number of "never tried before" reckless challenges and impresses all of the young people around him, earning him the title of "Maniac Magee".*

Running was not Maniac's only accomplishment. This story is filled with his friendships with Amanda Beale, a black girl; the Beale family, who took him in to stay with them; the Cobras and Mars Bar; and Grayson, the gruff but kindly old man who became like a father to him. Besides his legendary running, Maniac performs other amazing feats (like untangling Cobble's Knot) that earn him respect and admiration in this racially divided small town.

Suggestions for Further Reading

OTHER BOOKS BY JERRY SPINELLI

Space Station Seventh Grade © 1982

Fourth Grade Rats © 1991

Wringer © 1997

Stargirl © 2000

Loser © 2002

Jake and Lily © 2012

Hokey Pokey © 2013

OTHER RECOMMENDED RESOURCES

Betsy Byars, ***The Summer of the Swans*** © 1970

Katherine Paterson, ***The Great Gilly Hopkins*** © 1978

Patricia MacLachlan, ***Skylark*** © 1994

Louis Sachar, ***Holes*** © 1998

Richard Peck, ***A Year Down Yonder*** © 2000

Gary Paulsen, ***Brian's Hunt*** © 2003

Ria Voros, ***Nobody's Dog*** © 2012

List of Vocabulary

CHAPTERS 1 TO 5

• suspicious • encyclopedia • varsity • spiraling • punt • commotion • hoisted • goggle • hallucination • phantom

CHAPTERS 6 TO 10

• scanned • official • whiff • gangplank • beeline • pandemonium • demon • boulevard • maniac • blemish

CHAPTERS 11 TO 14

• prospects • asphalt • solemnly • sauerkraut • hemisphere • solution • crowbar • blotches • allergic • solitude

CHAPTERS 15 TO 21

• gawked • coot • hibernating • incubating • eons • pickpocket • testimony • opponent • distraction • confetti

CHAPTERS 22 TO 25

• zep • spree • claptrap • recognition • notion • dumbfounded • robust • rookies • sleazy • immortality

CHAPTERS 26 TO 32

• repertoire • geezer • portable • pommel • preposterous • traditional • mammoth • languished • meandering • stoic • blarney • knack • pantry • filigreed • lavatory • pallbearers

CHAPTERS 33 TO 35

• solitary • desolation • replicas • saltines • retaliated • trekking • urchins • lambasting • carrion • nonchalantly

CHAPTERS 36 TO 39

• blundered • marauding • tuition • perilous • megaphoned • marooned • pistoning • hysterical • exuberance • reunion

CHAPTERS 40 TO 43

• fortified • extort • shenanigans • chaotic • protruding • stogie • goading • swagger • sauntered • illusion

CHAPTERS 44 TO 46

• random • dovetailed • veered • congregations • slathered • trestle • amplified • constellations • wrenching • rasping

Jerry Spinelli

Born February 1st, 1941 in Norristown, Pennsylvania, Jerry Spinelli did not plan to be an author as his future career. His first love was to be a major league football player. At age sixteen, he wrote a poem about a football victory. His father thought it was so well done that—unknown to Jerry—he sent it to a local newspaper and it was published. When Jerry realized that he was not going to make it in football to the major leagues, he decided to become a writer instead.

Spinelli graduated from Gettysburg College, Pennsylvania in 1963. While a student there, he wrote short stories and was the editor of the college magazine. After he graduated, he became a writer and editor for a department store magazine. During the next twenty years, Jerry worked at ordinary jobs during the day so he would have the energy to write fiction in his spare time. Like many writers, he also wrote during his lunch breaks, at night and on weekends.

His career as a children's author began in 1982 with the publication of *Space Station Grade Seven.* He became a very productive writer and has a long list of titles to his credit. His stories contain a sense of humor and vocabulary easily understood by teens and young adults.

Spinelli's books for children have won recognition and awards: *Maniac Magee* won the Newbery Award in 1991 and *Wringer* won the Newbery Honor in 1998. All of his stories reflect his understanding of young people and their relationships with others.

Did You Know?

- **Jerry Spinelli's first four novels were written for adults, and all four were rejected by publishers.**
- **His fifth novel was intended for adults, but the publisher wanted it to be marketed as a young adult book. This novel, *Space Station Seventh Grade*, was published in 1982.**
- **Jerry Spinelli's wife, Eileen Mesi, is also an author of children's books.**

NAME: ______________________

Chapters One to Five

Answer the questions in complete sentences.

1. The title of this story is ***Maniac Magee***. What does "maniac" mean? What are some possible story ideas that could relate to the title?

____

____

____

2. This story is about a young boy who is often on his own in the world. What are some problems that he might face?

____

____

____

Vocabulary

Complete each sentence with a word from the list.

suspicious	**encyclopedia**	**varsity**	**spiraling**	**punt**
commotion	**hoisted**	**goggle**	**hallucination**	**phantom**

1. A lot of noise and confusion is called a ______________.

2. A book containing all kinds of information is called ___________.

3. To stare with rolling or bulging eyes is to ______________.

4. If you can't believe what you are seeing, you might be having a ______________.

5. I couldn't get up on the horse by myself so my cousin ___________ me.

6. Another word for a ghost is a ______________.

7. A kick given to a football before it touches the ground is called a ______________.

8. If an object is spinning in a circular pattern, we say it is ______________.

9. I doubt Jack's story; some of the details are very ______________.

10. As a very successful high school football player, Joe may go on to play at a _________.

After You Read

NAME: ______________________________

Chapters One to Five

1. Circle T if the statement is TRUE or F if it is FALSE.

T F a) Maniac Magee was an orphan whose real name was Jeffrey Lionel Magee.

T F b) Jeffrey hid out in an old barn for two years.

T F c) Amanda Beale and Jeffrey became friends right away.

T F d) Amanda agreed to lend Jeffrey one of her precious books.

T F e) Jeffrey caught a football pass meant for "Hands" Down.

T F f) Finsterwald was the kindest old man in the neighborhood.

2. **Number the events from 1 to 6 in the order they occurred in these chapters.**

☐ a) Jeffrey ran away; running for one year and covering 200 miles.

☐ b) Jeffrey stretched out on Finsterwald's front steps and began to read his book.

☐ c) The football players were dazzled when Jeffrey caught a football away from a star player, "Hands" Down.

☐ d) Jeffrey began screaming during the school spring musical.

☐ e) Jeffrey rescued Arnold Jones from Finsterwald's backyard.

☐ f) Jeffrey met Amanda, a black girl, who carried all of her books in a suitcase.

NAME: ______________________________

Chapters One to Five

Answer each question with a complete sentence.

1. When Jeffrey ran away from his aunt and uncle, it was a very impulsive action. What are some dangers of impulsive behavior?

2. What is "The Lost Year"?

3. Why did Jeffrey pick Two Mills as a stopping place from his running?

4. Why did Amanda say "But *you* can't come there. You can't even be here." ?

5. Why were the football players so stunned by the events on the field?

6. Why was Jeffrey called "the phantom Samaritan" for what happened at Finsterwald's house?

Pretend you are Jeffrey Lionel Magee. Tell how you became an orphan and why you ran away from your aunt and uncle's home. What did you plan to do once you reached Two Mills? Tell about meeting Amanda (and her books); about catching and returning the football; and about rescuing Arnold Jones from Finsterwald's backyard.

Before You Read

NAME: ______________________

Chapters Six to Ten

Answer the questions in complete sentences.

1. Jeffrey Magee is a runaway. What are some dangers of being a runaway?

____

____

2. If you were a runaway, how would you solve the problems of having enough food to eat and having some place to sleep?

____

____

Vocabulary

With a straight line, connect each word on the left with its meaning on the right.

1	**scanned**	A stain, a spot or a scar	A
2	**pandemonium**	A movable bridge used in getting on and off a ship	B
3	**official**	Wild disorder and confusion	C
4	**demon**	Another word for "devil"	D
5	**whiff**	Looked at closely; examined	E
6	**boulevard**	Having authority; agreed upon as right	F
7	**gangplank**	An insane or crazy person	G
8	**maniac**	A sudden light puff or smell	H
9	**beeline**	A wide street	I
10	**blemish**	The straightest way or line between two places	J

NAME: ________________________________

Chapters Six to Ten

1. Put a check mark (✓) next to the answer that is most correct.

a) Mrs. Pickwell called her children home for dinner by:
- ◯ **A** calling their cell phones.
- ◯ **B** standing on her porch and calling their names.
- ◯ **C** whistling to them.
- ◯ **D** sending the youngest child to find everyone.

b) John McNab was:
- ◯ **A** a scrawny, black kid.
- ◯ **B** a giant of a kid who could strike out any batter.
- ◯ **C** the umpire for the Little League.
- ◯ **D** a handyman for the park.

c) When the kid hit the ball, it:
- ◯ **A** flew up in the air and landed a few feet from home plate.
- ◯ **B** cleared the fence at the end of the field.
- ◯ **C** bounced off as a foul ball.
- ◯ **D** made a beeline right to McNab's head.

d) Instead of a ball, McNab tried to trick the kid by using:
- ◯ **A** a frog.
- ◯ **B** a clump of hard dirt.
- ◯ **C** an apple.
- ◯ **D** a rock.

e) Jeffrey Lionel Magee was now known as:
- ◯ **A** Sure Hit Magee.
- ◯ **B** Socker Magee.
- ◯ **C** Crazy Man Magee.
- ◯ **D** Maniac Magee.

f) Jeffrey was rescued from a fight with Mars Bar by:
- ◯ **A** the Cobras.
- ◯ **B** Mrs. Pickwell.
- ◯ **C** a black lady with a broom.
- ◯ **D** a police officer.

After You Read

NAME: ____________________

Chapters Six to Ten

Answer each question with a complete sentence.

1. How did Jeffrey manage to eat dinner at the Pickwell's house?

____

2. Do you think Mrs. Pickwell would have let him stay if she had known he was there? Why?

____

____

3. **a)** Why do you think Jeffrey decided to join the baseball game?

____

____

b) Why was McNab so determined to strike out Jeffrey?

____

4. Explain how Jeffrey came to be known as Maniac.

____

5. Reread the part where McNab and Maniac were facing off over the book. Illustrate your idea of this scene. Include the lady with the broom who rescues Maniac and sends him on his way.

In your journal entry today, write about your encounter with John McNab. Describe his appearance and his mannerisms. Tell how you came to join the game; the crowd's reaction when you hit the pitch he threw; the next three home runs; and the incident with the frog. Tell how you ended your time as a player in John McNab's game.

NAME: ______________________________

Chapters Eleven to Fourteen

Answer the questions in complete sentences.

1. Maniac is on his own and living in an unusual situation. List three things that are different between your world and Maniac's. Think about your family, your home, where you live, your school, your friends etc.

Maniac's Life	My Life
1.	
2.	
3.	
4.	

Vocabulary

Match each meaning with a word from the list.

prospects	**asphalt**	**solemnly**	**sauerkraut**	**hemisphere**
solution	**crowbar**	**blotches**	**allergic**	**solitude**

______ **1.** Being very sensitive to a substance; having a reaction.

______ **2.** Dark-colored, tar-like substance used for paving roads.

______ **3.** Large red spots usually on one's skin.

______ **4.** A strong iron or steel bar used for prying up things.

______ **5.** Half of the earth's surface.

______ **6.** Anything one expects or looks forward to.

______ **7.** Finely cut cabbage that is pickled in brine.

______ **8.** Seriously, gravely.

______ **9.** Loneliness; a quiet, lonely state or place.

______ **10.** An explanation or answer to a problem.

After You Read

NAME: ____________________

Chapters Eleven to Fourteen

1. Match each quote with the name of the character who said it.

[ ] **a)** "You runnin' from us. You afraid."

[ ] **b)** "Who ripped my book?"

[ ] **c)** "Don't you think it's about time you're heading home, Jeffrey?"

[ ] **d)** "Jeffrey! Jeffrey! Get a bath with us! Will ya?"

[ ] **e)** "Can't be that. Can you imagine a youngster getting sick on pizza?"

[ ] **f)** "Hey, everybody! Member I said 'bout the little white dude snatched the pass off me in gym class? Here he is. This is the dude!"

2. Complete each sentence with an explanation of why it happened.

a) Mars Bar's eyes went as big as headlights because ____________________
____________________.

b) Amanda screeched at her Mom for telling what she said about Jeffrey because ____
____________________.

c) Mrs. Beale said that Jeffrey should be heading home because ____________________
____________________.

d) Maniac Magee finally had an address because ____________________
____________________.

e) Jeffrey didn't realize he might be allergic to pizza because ____________________
____________________.

NAME: ______________________

Chapters Eleven to Fourteen

Answer each question with a complete sentence.

1. How do you think Jeffrey felt when Amanda showed up and confronted Mars Bar? Give reasons for your answer.

____

____

____

2. How did Mr. Beale react when he realized that Jeffrey had no home?

____

____

3. List eight chores Jeffrey did while at the Beale's house.

____

____

____

____

4. Describe Jeffrey's experience of going to church.

____

____

5. When everyone started calling him Maniac, why was Jeffrey afraid of losing his real name?

____

____

____

In your journal entry today, tell how you feel about moving into the Beale household. Include your time with the little ones and your feelings toward the other family members. Tell what it feels like to "have an address", a family who cares about you, about going to church and the Fourth of July block party. Then tell how you will react when the time comes that you can no longer stay there.

NAME: ______________________

Chapters Fifteen to Twenty-One

Answer the questions in complete sentences.

1. In this section, Maniac's fame spread all over the East End. Think about what it would be like to be famous. List three pros and three cons of being a famous person.

Pros	Cons
1.	
2.	
3.	

2. Also in this section, Maniac is confronted with **discrimination**. What are some ways that people discriminate against other people?

____

____

Vocabulary

Match each meaning with a word from the list!

gawked	coot	hibernating	incubating	eons
pickpocket	testimony	opponent	distraction	confetti

1. A slang term meaning "an old fool".
2. Very long periods of time.
3. Stared with one's mouth open.
4. Small bits of colored paper.
5. A person who is on the other side.
6. A statement used for proof.
7. Sitting on eggs to hatch them.
8. A person who steals from your pocket.
9. Taking away one's attention.
10. Spending the winter sleeping.

NAME: ______________________________

Chapters Fifteen to Twenty-One

1. Circle T if the statement is TRUE or F if it is FALSE.

T F a) Mrs. Beal sent Maniac to his room for talking trash to her.

T F b) Maniac didn't see any difference between the whites and the people of color.

T F c) Maniac was the target of discrimination when someone wrote on the brick wall.

T F d) Cobble's Knot is a contest for fancy knot tying.

T F e) Cobble's Knot had defeated many challengers.

T F f) Everyone held a celebration party to mark Maniac's success.

2. Number the events from 1 to 6 in the order they occurred in the chapters.

☐ a) Amanda's beloved "A" book was torn to shreds.

☐ b) An old man told Maniac to return to his own kind.

☐ c) Untangling Cobble's Knot turned Maniac into a neighborhood hero.

☐ d) The Cobras and a group of East Enders escorted Maniac out of town.

☐ e) Maniac learned not to talk trash to Mrs. Beale.

☐ f) Amanda tried to talk Maniac out of leaving town.

After You Read

NAME: ____________________

Chapters Fifteen to Twenty-One

Answer each question with a complete sentence.

1. Maniac is thrilled to be living with the Beale family and they treated him like one of their own children. But trouble is growing in the neighborhood. In your own words explain these sentences: "Maniac loved almost everything about his new life. But everything did not love him back."

____

____

2. Reread the section where the old man confronts Maniac and tells him to leave and go back home to his own kind.

a) Why do you think the old man is behaving this way?

____

____

b) How does Maniac react to the old man's words?

____

____

3. **Irony** occurs in a story when one action results in another unexpected and opposite event. What is the irony of the prize that Maniac receives for untangling the Knot?

____

____

4. "Maniac Magee walked --- not ran --- right out of town." What do you predict Maniac will do next?

____

____

____

In your journal entry, write a detailed account of your amazing feat of untangling Cobble's Knot. Begin with Amanda's idea for you to attempt it. Describe the Knot and your first impressions as to whether you could untangle it. Include the part where you take a nap and the crowd's reaction to your doing so. Finally describe the scene that followed your success in conquering the Knot.

NAME: ______________________________

Chapters Twenty-Two to Twenty-Five

Answer the questions in complete sentences.

1. In this section, Maniac meets Grayson, an old groundskeeper at the Elmwood Park Zoo.

a) What might this meeting mean for Maniac?

____

____

____

b) What are some things that Maniac could do for Grayson?

____

____

____

Vocabulary

Choose a word from the list that means the same or nearly the same as the underlined words.

zep	spree	claptrap	recognition	notion
dumbfounded	robust	rookies	sleazy	immortality

1. The politician's promises were just **a lot of empty talk.**
2. We were **full of disbelief** when we heard the story.
3. Our dog had the **silly idea** that he could win a fight with a porcupine.
4. For lunch we had a **delicious sandwich**.
5. A lumberjack has to be **strong and healthy** to do his job.
6. Our baseball team has a lot of **young and inexperienced players**.
7. My grandfather received an award of **acknowledgement** for his service.
8. The old beggar's clothes were **flimsy, dirty and tattered**.
9. Some rock stars think that they will have **fame that lasts forever**.
10. If I won the lottery, I would go on a shopping **marathon**.

After You Read

NAME: ______________________________

Chapters Twenty-Two to Twenty-Five

1. Put a check mark (✓) next to the answer that is most correct.

a) After Maniac left the Beale's house, he was living:
- ◯ **A** in an apartment in the West End.
- ◯ **B** back at his aunt and uncle's house.
- ◯ **C** in a lean-to near the buffaloes at the zoo.
- ◯ **D** in a shelter for the homeless.

b) What did Grayson do after he found Maniac?
- ◯ **A** He woke him up and told him to move out of there.
- ◯ **B** He picked him up and carried him to the band shell.
- ◯ **C** He drove him back to the Beale's house.
- ◯ **D** He left him there and went back to work.

c) Grayson was surprised when Maniac said he had lived in the East End because:
- ◯ **A** it was a very long way from the zoo.
- ◯ **B** only rich people lived there and Maniac was poor.
- ◯ **C** he knew a lot of people who lived in the East End and he didn't recognize Maniac.
- ◯ **D** only black people lived there and Maniac was white.

d) After feeding Maniac, Grayson made him:
- ◯ **A** take a shower and put on clean clothes.
- ◯ **B** go to the barber for a haircut.
- ◯ **C** go shopping for new shoes.
- ◯ **D** go back to the buffalo pen.

e) Maniac says he is not going to school because:
- ◯ **A** he has finished all his grades.
- ◯ **B** he doesn't want to make new friends.
- ◯ **C** he doesn't have time for school.
- ◯ **D** school and a home go together and he has no home address.

f) When Maniac asked Grayson what he wanted to be when he grew up, he said:
- ◯ **A** a fireman.
- ◯ **B** a policeman.
- ◯ **C** a baseball player.
- ◯ **D** head zookeeper.

NAME: ______________________

Chapters Twenty-Two to Twenty-Five

Answer each question with a complete sentence.

1. In your own words, describe what Maniac looked like when Grayson found him.

____

____

____

2. Think about how Grayson treats Maniac when he finds him. What kind of a man do you think he is? Give reasons for your answer.

____

____

____

3. Reread the sections that detail Grayson's baseball career in the Minor Leagues. Retell the story by describing six major events in the story. Write your answers on the chart below.

Event #	My description of the event
1	
2	
3	
4	
5	
6	

In today's entry, tell about the growing relationship between you (Maniac) and Grayson. Include your opinion of Grayson and how he treats you. Tell what you think of the stories he tells you.

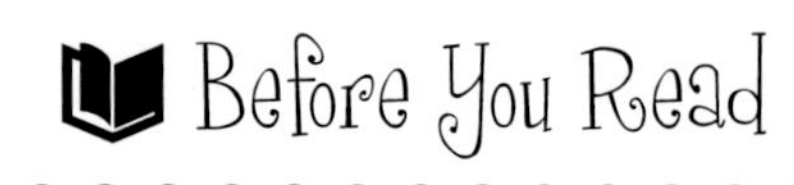

NAME: ______________________

Chapters Twenty-Six to Thirty-Two

Vocabulary

blarney
filigreed
geezer
knack
languished
lavatory
mammoth
meandering
pallbearers
pommel
portable
preposterous
repertoire
stoic
traditional

Across	Down
2. Drooping or lingering.	1. Huge or gigantic.
6. Easily carried or moved.	3. Indifferent, self-controlled.
7. Synonym for "customary".	4. Slang term for "old person".
8. Ridiculous or absurd.	5. A special skill for doing something.
9. Synonym for excessive flattery.	6. People who carry the coffin at a funeral.
11. Wandering aimlessly.	10. A list of skills or actions that one could perform.
12. To beat with one's fists.	
13. Synonym for "toilet or bathroom".	
14. Very delicate and lacelike pattern.	

NAME: ______________________________

Chapters Twenty-Six to Thirty-Two

1. Circle **T** if the statement is TRUE or **F** if it is FALSE.

T F **a)** Maniac could hit the "stopball" right out of the park.

T F **b)** Grayson had never learned how to read.

T F **c)** Maniac encouraged Grayson to read by using "baseball talk".

T F **d)** Maniac had never learned how to cook.

T F **e)** Grayson and Maniac celebrated Thanksgiving in fine style.

T F **f)** 101 Band Shell Boulevard was Maniac's official new address.

T F **g)** Maniac ran to get help as soon as he realized Grayson had died.

T F **h)** All of Grayson's friends came to his funeral.

2. **Number the events from 1 to 7 in the order they occurred in the chapters.**

☐ **a)** Grayson gave Maniac his precious old baseball glove as a Christmas gift.

☐ **b)** Maniac and Grayson celebrated Thanksgiving with a huge chicken dinner with all the trimmings.

☐ **c)** Maniac taught Grayson how to read books like *The Little Engine That Could* and *Mike Mulligan's Steam Shovel.*

☐ **d)** Grayson passed away in his sleep. Maniac was the only mourner at the funeral.

☐ **e)** Grayson stayed overnight with Maniac in the band shell room.

☐ **f)** Grayson taught Maniac a number of baseball skills but he never learned how to hit the "stopball."

☐ **g)** Grayson moved in with Maniac. They decorated their home for Christmas.

NAME: ____________________

Chapters Twenty-Six to Thirty-Two

Answer each question with a complete sentence.

1. In these chapters, we learn more about the personalities of the characters. Read the descriptions for each character. Find proof in the story of that quality and record it on the chart.

Character	**Quality**	**Proof from the story**
Maniac	**1.** caring	**1.**
	2. determined	**2.**
	3. funny	**3.**
Grayson	**1.** caring	**1.**
	2. generous	**2.**
	3. contented	**3.**

2. When Grayson dies, Maniac is in shock.

a) How does Maniac react? What are some of the things he does?

____

____

b) Why do you think Maniac does these things? Give reasons for your opinion.

____

____

3. While waiting for the minister, Maniac makes a decision to do something. What does he decide to do? Why do you think he decided to do this?

____

____

Write an entry about all of the great times you had with Grayson: learning baseball tips, teaching him to read, celebrating Thanksgiving and Christmas. Then tell about discovering that Grayson had died during the night and how you felt.

NAME: ______________________

Chapters Thirty-Three to Thirty-Five

Answer the questions in complete sentences.

1. Part III begins the next phase of Maniac's life. Read the following statement from this part. "Even if the Superintendent had allowed it, he could not have brought himself to stay at the band shell."

a) It is January and Maniac has nowhere else to go. Why do you think he will not stay there?

____

____

b) What are some possible choices of places where Maniac could stay?

____

____

2. How is Maniac unfortunate in his relationships with other people?

____

____

Vocabulary

Match each meaning with a word from the list.

solitary	desolation	replicas	saltines	retaliated
trekking	urchins	lambasting	carrion	nonchalantly

	1.	Traveling along slowly.
	2.	Lonely, sad, or feeling hopeless.
	3.	Hitting or beating.
	4.	A kind of cracker.
	5.	Indifferent or acting without any cares.
	6.	All alone, singular.
	7.	Poor and ragged children.
	8.	Copies or reproductions.
	9.	Dead and decaying flesh.
	10.	Got even or fought back.

After You Read

NAME: ______________________________

Chapters Thirty-Three to Thirty-Five

1. **Circle T if the statement is TRUE or F if it is FALSE.**

T F a) The weather was so cold that Maniac decided to return to the band shell for shelter.

T F b) Maniac ate at soup kitchens and did odd jobs for housewives in order to survive.

T F c) Three small boys were hiding in the cabin near Maniac.

T F d) Maniac treated the boys to pizza using his prize certificate.

T F e) Giant John recognized Maniac as "the frog man".

T F f) Maniac told a story about John's secret pitch so he wouldn't be disgraced in front of his family.

T F g) The McNab family is very similar to the Beale family.

2. A **simile** is a comparison between two things using the words "like", "as" or "seems". A **metaphor** is a comparison that uses no connecting words. In your own words, explain the meaning of each of these expressions from the story. Identify each expression as a simile or a metaphor.

Expression from the Story	Meaning	Simile or Metaphor
a) In his mind's eye, he saw the red and yellow trolley careening from the high track.		
b) January slipped an icy finger under his collar.		
c) Which, of course, got Giant John more than a little steamed.		
d) They tore into the bag like jackals into carrion.		

NAME: ______________________

After You Read

Chapters Thirty-Three to Thirty-Five

Answer each question with a complete sentence.

1. Maniac has overcome many obstacles and still has managed to survive. In this section we see him in a different state of mind.

a) What has caused this change in his outlook on life?

____

____

b) What does Maniac decide to do? What does this tell you about his state of mind?

____

____

2. Describe the first meeting between Maniac and the two young boys.

____

____

3. Why do you think Maniac persuaded the young boys to go back home?

____

____

4. **a)** Why do you think the old man is behaving this way?

____

b) How does Maniac react to this confusion?

____

____

Today you thought about how hopeless your life had become. Tell why you think that way. Give an example from the story if you wish. You made a decision that you would stay in the cabin and wait for death to come. Tell what happened to distract you from that decision. How did you convince the boys to go home? Briefly describe their living conditions and your impressions of the house and the people living there.

NAME: ____________________

Chapters Thirty-Six to Thirty-Nine

Answer the questions in complete sentences.

1. We have learned that the McNab boys didn't like school and often didn't bother to go. Maniac decided to find ways to bribe them. He gave them his pizza prize and that worked for a while. If you were in Maniac's place, what are some things you would use to get the boys to go to school? Try to think of things the boys would really like to have.

____

2. Jerry Spinelli likes to use **exaggeration** to make a point. Read these sentences from the story.

"For ten minutes, fifteen kids --- and possibly the universe --- held their breath. The only sounds were inside their heads --- the moaning and wailing of the ghosts of all the poor slobs who had ever blundered onto Finsterwald's property."

Explain in your own words two examples of **exaggeration** found in these sentences.

____

____

Vocabulary

With a straight line, connect each word on the left with its meaning on the right.

1	blundered	Coming together again	A
2	marooned	Dangerous; very hazardous	B
3	marauding	Unable to stop laughing, crying; extremely upset	C
4	pistoning	Plundering or stealing	D
5	tuition	Left in a lonely, helpless spot	E
6	hysterical	Made a big, stupid mistake	F
7	perilous	Moving rapidly up and down	G
8	exuberance	Money paid for schooling	H
9	reunion	Overflowing, lavish	I

NAME: ______________________

Chapters Thirty-Six to Thirty-Nine

1. Put a check mark (✓) next to the answer that is most correct.

a) If Russell and Piper went to school the rest of the week, Maniac would:
- ◯ **A** take them to see an action movie.
- ◯ **B** teach them how to untie hard knots.
- ◯ **C** take them to the East End with him.
- ◯ **D** show them a shortcut to Mexico on Saturday.

b) When Maniac knocked on Finsterwald's front door, the boys expected that:
- ◯ **A** Mr. Finsterwald would invite him in for a visit.
- ◯ **B** no one would answer the door.
- ◯ **C** he would be pulled into the house never to be seen again.
- ◯ **D** there would be a loud gruff noise from within the house.

c) One "heroic feat" performed by Maniac was:
- ◯ **A** he hit a telephone pole with a stone sixty-six times in a row.
- ◯ **B** he tucked his arm, all the way up to his shoulder, into a mysterious hole by the creek.
- ◯ **C** he climbed into the buffalo pen and hugged the baby buffalo.
- ◯ **D** he walked barefoot through a rat-infested dump.

d) When Maniac heard Mars Bar's loud voice,:
- ◯ **A** he yelled right back at him.
- ◯ **B** he pretended he didn't hear him.
- ◯ **C** he ran away back across the street.
- ◯ **D** he started running toward Mars Bar.

e) Mars Bar said that Maniac cheated in the race because:
- ◯ **A** the crowd had interfered with Mars Bar's path.
- ◯ **B** the starter had let Maniac go first.
- ◯ **C** Maniac really had cheated.
- ◯ **D** he was mad that Maniac had beat him.

f) George McNab was turning his house into a fort because:
- ◯ **A** he likes to keep the boys busy.
- ◯ **B** he wants to be ready for any severe weather.
- ◯ **C** he thinks the blacks are going to invade their neighborhood.
- ◯ **D** he saw the idea on a tv show.

After You Read

NAME: ______________________

Chapters Thirty-Six to Thirty-Nine

Answer each question with a complete sentence.

1. Maniac has become a legend in the neighborhood.

a) What does it mean to "become a legend"?

____

b) Why do you think Maniac continues to perform "heroic feats"?

____

____

c) Why do the neighborhood kids think these are such "heroic feats"?

____

____

2. "And then one day they gave him the most perilous challenge of all. They dared him to go into the East End."

a) Why is this "the most perilous challenge of all"?

____

____

b) Why would the kids pick this challenge for Maniac?

____

____

3. Maniac returned to the McNab's house but he realized that he could not stay there. What do you think he will do next and where do you think he will go?

____

____

Tell the story of the race with Mars Bar. Where was the race held? Why did you agree to it? What did they use for a finish line? Why weren't you sure that winning was the best plan? Why did you decide to turn around and race backwards? Why do you think other boys challenged you to a race with them? Why were you so glad to see Hester and Lester?

NAME: ______________________

Chapters Forty to Forty-Three

Answer the question in a complete sentence.

1. Maniac appears to use running as an escape from the pressures of his life. What are some other ways that people relieve stress in their lives?

____

____

____

Vocabulary

Write a complete sentence using the following words. Make sure that the meaning of each word is clear in your sentence.

Fortified ______________________

Stogie ______________________

Extort ______________________

Goading ______________________

Shenanigans ______________________

Swagger ______________________

Chaotic ______________________

Sauntered ______________________

Protruding ______________________

Illusion ______________________

After You Read

NAME: ______________________

Chapters Forty to Forty-Three

1. **Figurative language** is used to give us a different look at a simple idea. Explain the meaning of these phrases in your own words.

a) "treated him like a legend in the flesh" ______________________
______________________.

b) "He popped off for a good ten minutes" ______________________
______________________.

c) "from the rip-stone-evil scowl on his face" ______________________
______________________.

d) "Maniac could feel the voltage that surged through Mars Bar" ______________________
______________________.

e) "The laughter stopped as if cut by scissors" ______________________
______________________.

2. **Imagery** refers to phrases or words that help us to imagine what a person or thing is like. It helps us to form a mental picture of a situation: sights, sounds, feelings. Reread the section starting "And that was only the half of it." as far as "before anyone could reach for anything". Write examples of imagery and tell how they appeal to our senses. For example: "the kid swaggered in", from the way he walked we can feel he is confident.

____
____
____
____
____
____
____
____
____

Chapters Forty to Forty-Three

Answer each question with a complete sentence.

1. **a)** Maniac returned to the McNab house and tried to influence the two young boys. What rewards did he give to try to get them to go to school?

____

____

b) "It was a maddening, chaotic time for Maniac". Why do you think he stayed at the McNabs?

____

____

2. Maniac came up with the idea that if the McNabs could actually have a black person in their home, they might change some of their opinions about black people. Why do you think he chose Mars Bar to take to the party? Was his choice a good one? Why?

____

____

3. Reread the section that describes the game "Rebels". Illustrate how this scene may have looked. Add speech bubbles for your characters.

Explain your idea to take Mars Bar to the McNab boys' birthday party. How did you plan to trick Mars Bar into going? What did you think you could accomplish by taking him to the McNabs? Can you really change people's beliefs so easily? Give your opinion of how successful that plan turned out.

NAME: ____________________

Chapters Forty-Four to Forty-Six

Answer the questions in complete sentences.

1. In this section, the story will reach some kind of conclusion. What do you think that conclusion will be?

____

____

____

2. Maniac has made a number of friends but he has not settled into any one family. Why do you think that is? Give reasons for your opinion.

____

____

____

Vocabulary

Complete each sentence with a word from the list.

random	trestle	dovetailed	amplified	veered
constellations	congregations	wrenching	slathered	rasping

a) My little cousin loves astronomy. He knows the names of 10 __________.

b) The sun was so hot that we __________ on sunscreen to protect our skin.

c) The truck went into the ditch after it __________ off the gravel road.

d) Winning the lottery is really just __________ luck.

e) The __________ of many churches assembled to remember the town hero.

f) When we heard that __________ voice coming out of the darkness, we ran for home!

g) The speakers __________ the music to an ear-splitting level.

h) The football player gained control of the ball by __________ it away from his opponent.

i) We could hear the train rattling along on the old __________.

j) Well-made wooden furniture has __________ corners.

NAME: ______________________________

Chapters Forty-Four to Forty-Six

1. **Circle T if the statement is TRUE or F if it is FALSE.**

T F **a)** Mars Bar wanted to run with Maniac so he could beat him in a race.

T F **b)** Maniac rushed to save Russell who was hanging onto the trestle.

T F **c)** Maniac returned to the buffalo lean to have a sleep.

T F **d)** Maniac confided to Mars Bar about his childhood.

T F **e)** The McNab boys refused to let Mars Bar's mother help them.

T F **f)** Amanda came looking for Maniac and planned to take him home with her.

2. **Number the events from 1 to 12 in the order they occurred in these chapters.**

☐ **a)** Maniac turned and walked away.

☐ **b)** One morning, Piper came to them, crying and asking for help.

☐ **c)** Amanda took Maniac back to her house to stay.

☐ **d)** Maniac was out running early one morning when he met Mars Bar running too.

☐ **e)** Mars Bar wanted to know why Maniac didn't try to rescue Russell.

☐ **f)** Mars Bar asked Maniac why he never visits his house.

☐ **g)** Maniac was frozen on the spot.

☐ **h)** Mars Bar got Amanda Beale to come to the buffalo pen with him to see Maniac.

☐ **i)** Soon they were running side by side, silently, each day.

☐ **j)** Mars Bar looked for Maniac at the buffalo pen.

☐ **k)** Maniac told Mars Bar the story of how his parents died.

☐ **l)** Piper's brother, Russell, was clinging to the trestle, too terrified to move.

After You Read

NAME: ______________________________

Chapters Forty-Four to Forty-Six

Answer each question with a complete sentence.

1. Why do you think Mars Bar decided to join Maniac in his daily run?

____

____

2. Describe how Piper McNab looked and sounded as he came down the street. Include at least five descriptive words or phrases.

____

____

____

3. Why was Mars Bar so amazed that Maniac seemed frozen on the spot instead of rushing to rescue Russell?

____

____

____

4. Up to this point, Maniac has not shared the story of his parents' death with anyone. Why do you think he decided to tell the story to Mars Bar?

____

____

5. In your opinion, does this story have a suitable ending? Did it end the way you thought it would? Give reasons for your opinion.

____

____

It seems as though your life is looking better and soon you will be a real part of a family that wants you. What are some changes that will take place in your life when you move in with the Beale family? What might be some problems that arise? Tell what you think the next year holds for you. Will you return to school? Will you continue to run? Try to think about some new activities you might get involved in.

Chapters 1 to 10

Story Summary Booklet

Sections 1 and 2 give us an introduction to the story and some background information.

Make a summary booklet in this way:

- Cut 10 strips of white paper 3 inches (8 cm) by 8 inches (20 cm) each.
- Number the strips: Chapter 1, Chapter 2, etc.
- On each strip of paper, write a sentence to tell the most important point in that chapter.
- Put your sentence strips in order and staple them together.
- Illustrate at least 5 of your sentences.

Share your Story Summary Booklet with your classmates.

Chapters 11 to 21

Writing a Limerick

A limerick is a poem that uses humor. It relies on rhythm and rhyme and generally discusses a person (character) and a place (setting). A limerick has five lines.

In this part of the story, Jeffrey becomes "Maniac Magee". Write a limerick about Maniac Magee.

It might begin "There once was a boy named Magee
Who ...."

A rhyming couplet has two lines that rhyme with each other. Write a poem about Amanda Beale or Mars Bar. Your poem should have at least four rhyming couplets.

Chapters 22 to 32

Dear Grayson

This part of the story introduces the character of Grayson, the gruff but kindly old man who became a father figure to Maniac. They had great times until Grayson suddenly died.

- Compose a letter that is written to Grayson from Maniac's point of view. Use first person "I".
- Describe your first meeting and your first impression of the old man.
- How you felt about living with him and sharing stories.
- The things you learned and the things you taught him.
- The importance of your Thanksgiving and Christmas celebrations.
- How you felt when he suddenly died.
- What you feel your life will be like now; things you will miss.

Chapters 33 to 39

Problem Solving

In most stories, the main character encounters problems that need to be solved.

Review the details of this section.

Identify one **major problem** and one **minor problem** that Maniac faced.

Write a paragraph for each problem to explain:

- What the problem was,
- Who caused the problem,
- How the problem was solved, and
- What Maniac learned from the situation.

Chapters 40 to 46

Stereotyping

A stereotype is a fixed idea or a prejudice held by a number of people or by a specific group of people. Sometimes people believe that any different group of people is inferior. Stereotypes can be based on people's gender, race, weight, economic status, how they dress or look, what language they speak or physical disability.

Construct a chart like this one on a separate sheet of paper.

Add four more features of your own. Then complete the chart with ideas of stereotypes.

Common Stereotypes

If people are	They must be
black	
white	
rich	
poor	

Chapters 1 to 46

Maniac's Time Capsule

A time capsule is a collection of items that are stored and left for a future person to open. Some things that are chosen to be placed into a time capsule might include:

- An item that is important to the person,
- A fad of the time,
- Something essential for living, and
- Personal photos, books, videos, notes, toys, newspapers.

Describe the items that you think Maniac Magee would place into a time capsule. State the reason for each of your choices.

Then, create a time capsule using the items you described in your story.

HINT: A box or plastic container makes a good "capsule".

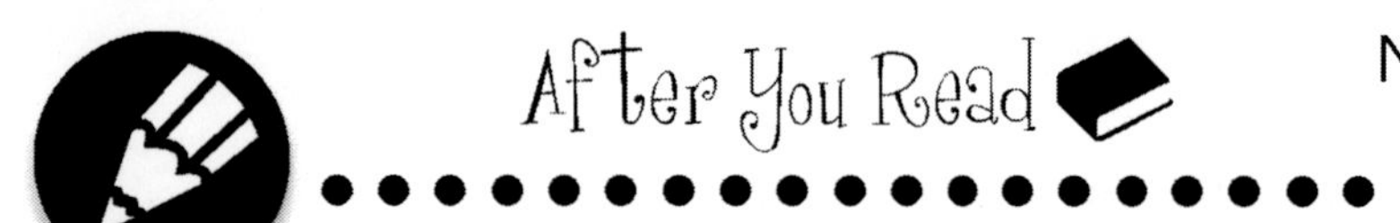

NAME: ______________________________

Word Search Puzzle

Find the following words from the story. The words are written horizontally, vertically, diagonally, and some are written backwards.

asphalt	**freedom**	**knack**	**pickpocket**	**urchins**
beeline	**geezer**	**lambasting**	**quietly**	**varsity**
coot	**hemisphere**	**maniac**	**random**	**wrenching**
desolation	**illusion**	**notion**	**stoic**	**young**
extort	**justice**	**opponent**	**trekking**	**zep**

d	j	y	n	p	a	r	e	i	l	h	f	r	q	n	k	t	n	f	j	d	b	e	q	v
f	u	o	t	z	q	s	n	b	s	e	s	s	a	n	o	o	n	l	r	a	g	n	h	l
d	s	z	i	i	a	o	o	s	u	l	t	l	a	r	i	t	m	e	q	e	w	o	e	i
f	t	b	v	t	s	l	p	n	b	c	r	c	u	t	l	w	i	u	n	a	e	r	u	m
w	i	a	l	j	c	r	d	s	c	u	k	u	a	a	u	e	i	o	u	o	e	d	u	w
j	c	l	i	g	d	i	a	e	b	g	d	l	h	r	v	e	f	l	n	z	p	a	o	l
l	e	a	m	h	v	t	d	v	l	g	o	p	e	b	t	d	x	s	e	v	e	p	a	m
e	a	t	w	u	f	r	f	r	a	s	s	b	k	l	p	v	h	e	g	n	q	e	o	r
p	a	m	l	g	g	o	c	t	e	a	e	x	y	j	d	u	g	e	b	k	e	a	r	a
i	x	g	b	p	r	t	v	d	s	t	n	a	e	r	c	o	r	p	e	h	a	z	a	n
c	e	u	e	a	o	x	c	i	o	t	s	c	a	r	n	o	i	s	u	l	l	i	d	d
k	g	z	w	u	s	e	v	z	n	a	y	i	z	a	p	s	q	c	t	q	u	q	l	o
p	w	h	c	g	g	t	e	h	e	g	c	s	p	d	t	n	m	u	u	v	q	m	a	m
o	h	t	l	m	m	c	i	a	u	j	h	u	r	l	y	b	u	r	l	y	l	u	a	b
c	b	e	e	l	i	n	e	n	w	l	g	a	h	a	e	a	x	e	a	q	e	x	g	a
k	s	n	i	h	c	r	u	r	g	m	a	n	i	a	c	n	u	s	l	d	u	u	o	n
e	k	c	c	d	r	d	e	v	c	b	g	a	u	g	s	a	t	q	n	o	m	t	t	a
t	i	l	g	f	a	n	n	l	q	u	h	a	g	o	c	d	d	e	w	l	c	d	u	d
u	d	e	k	r	c	m	w	z	w	m	s	t	n	t	y	j	g	h	o	o	d	g	k	j
q	p	n	l	h	l	e	u	i	a	v	x	h	i	o	p	g	y	u	i	u	i	y	t	g
h	m	s	i	u	v	n	i	l	t	l	m	j	k	o	m	e	g	e	s	r	s	g	s	e
e	f	n	h	e	m	i	s	p	h	e	r	e	k	c	l	v	q	l	y	e	z	q	k	v
u	g	o	z	q	h	s	u	b	e	f	a	c	e	s	o	r	u	g	g	u	c	u	a	r
u	e	n	c	x	k	r	h	y	i	a	i	a	r	k	b	m	r	e	d	i	g	r	a	m
h	f	s	u	l	s	d	l	g	s	q	s	f	t	a	b	p	s	r	e	a	j	s	c	p

NAME: ______________________

After You Read

Comprehension Quiz

32

Answer each question in a complete sentence.

1. Why did Jeffrey run away from his aunt and uncle? What was his plan for survival?

____

____

2

2. How do you know that Mrs. Pickwell is a generous person?

____

____

2

3. How did Jeffrey come to be called Maniac Magee?

____

____

____

5

4. How did staying with the Beale family change Maniac's life?

____

____

2

5. Why was Maniac so surprised by the old man's rant to tell him to go away?

____

____

2

6. What was the irony for Maniac in the prize he won for untangling Cobble's Knot?

____

____

2

7. What impact did becoming friends with Grayson have on Maniac's life?

____

____

2

SUBTOTAL: /17

After You Read

NAME: ______________________

Comprehension Quiz

8. Grayson told stories to Maniac and taught him some baseball tips. What did he want Maniac to teach him?

______________________ 1

9. How did Maniac react to Grayson's sudden death?

____

______________________ 4

____

10. Maniac decided to stay inside the little cabin until he died from exposure. Was that a realistic plan? Why?

______________________ 2

____

11. How would you describe life in the McNab household? Why did Maniac stay there?

______________________ 3

____

____

12. Why didn't Maniac rescue Russell from the trestle? 1

____

____

13. "Maniac always seemed to lose the people who meant the most to him." Explain this sentence and give examples to support your answer.

______________________ 2

____

14. Maniac lived with different people in different settings. In your opinion, which of his "homes" was the most suitable? Give a reason for your answer?

______________________ 2

____

SUBTOTAL: /15

11

1.

Maniac refers to someone who is crazy or insane.

2.

Answers will vary, but may include: finding food and shelter; being lonely; his safety

Vocabulary

1. commotion
2. encyclopedia
3. goggle
4. hallucination
5. hoisted
6. phantom
7. punt
8. spiraling
9. suspicious
10. varsity

12

1.

a) T
b) F
c) F
d) T
e) T
f) F

2.

a) 2
b) 6
c) 4
d) 1
e) 5
f) 3

13

1.

Answers will vary, but may include: You or others could get hurt; it's not safe.

2.

It is the time that Jeffrey spent running until he stopped at Two Mills.

3.

It was across the river from Bridgeport where he was born.

4.

Amanda lived in the East End where blacks live. Jeffrey is white so it is unsafe for him to even be there.

5.

A little kid caught the ball; ran up the field through the players; then threw the ball back.

6.

Jeffrey appeared out of nowhere (like a ghost) and rescued the boy and took him to safety.

14

1.

Answers will vary.

2.

Answers will vary.

Vocabulary

1. E
2. C
3. F
4. D
5. H
6. I
7. B
8. G
9. J
10. A

15

1.

a) C
b) B
c) C
d) A
e) D
f) C

16

1.

a) When Mrs. Pickwell whistled for the children, he joined them and went to eat.

b) Yes because the Pickwells often fed people who were down on their luck.

2.

Answers will vary but may include:

a) He was looking for some fun; he wanted to challenge McNab.

b) McNab struck out all batters and he wanted to keep his reputation.

3.

Everyone was talking about the new kid and the things he had done. Someone gave him the nickname.

4.

Answers will vary.

EZ✓

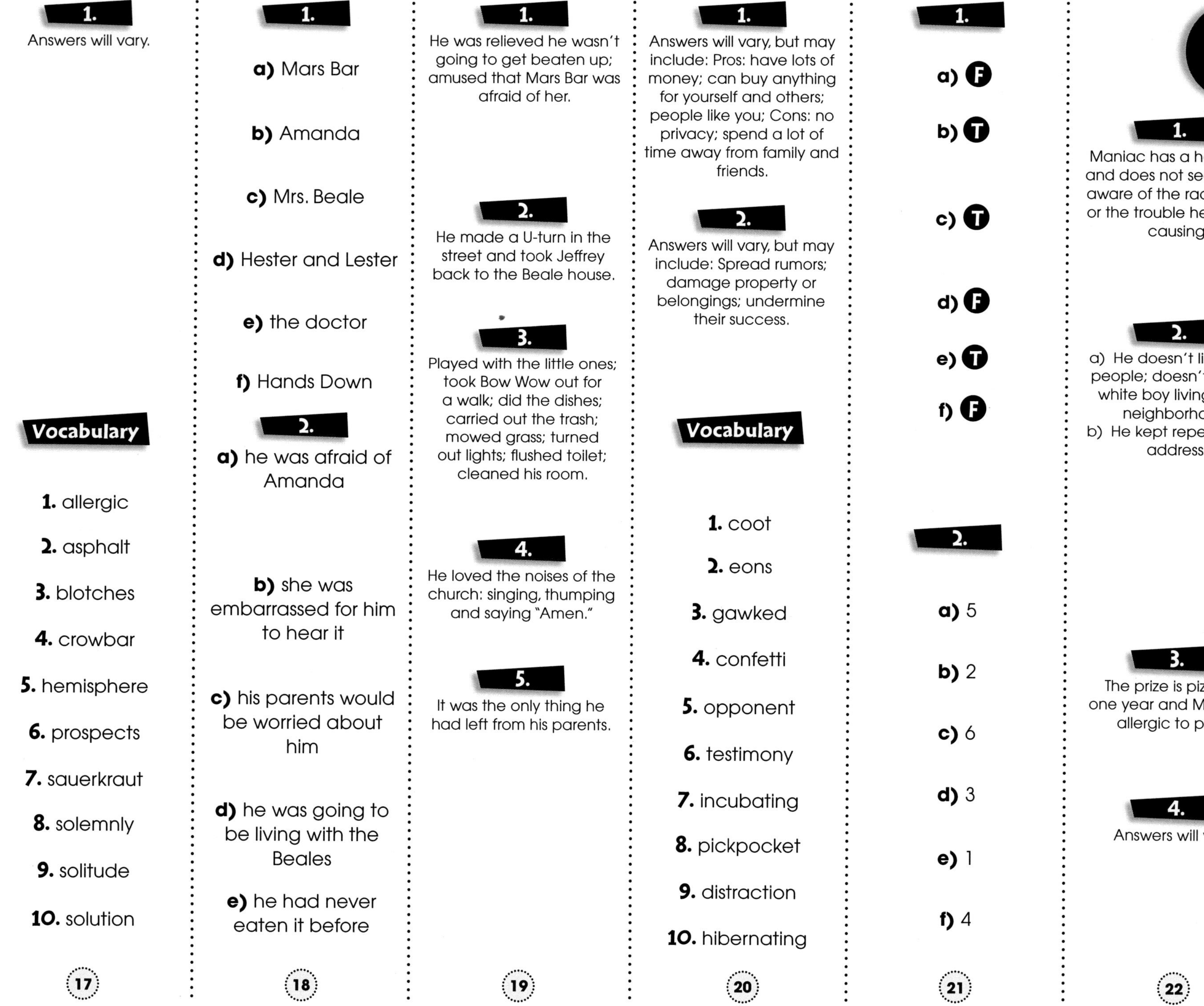

EZ✓

1.
Answers will vary.

Vocabulary

1. allergic
2. asphalt
3. blotches
4. crowbar
5. hemisphere
6. prospects
7. sauerkraut
8. solemnly
9. solitude
10. solution

17

1.

a) Mars Bar
b) Amanda
c) Mrs. Beale
d) Hester and Lester
e) the doctor
f) Hands Down

2.

a) he was afraid of Amanda
b) she was embarrassed for him to hear it
c) his parents would be worried about him
d) he was going to be living with the Beales
e) he had never eaten it before

18

1.
He was relieved he wasn't going to get beaten up; amused that Mars Bar was afraid of her.

2.
He made a U-turn in the street and took Jeffrey back to the Beale house.

3.
Played with the little ones; took Bow Wow out for a walk; did the dishes; carried out the trash; mowed grass; turned out lights; flushed toilet; cleaned his room.

4.
He loved the noises of the church: singing, thumping and saying "Amen."

5.
It was the only thing he had left from his parents.

19

1.
Answers will vary, but may include: Pros: have lots of money; can buy anything for yourself and others; people like you; Cons: no privacy; spend a lot of time away from family and friends.

2.
Answers will vary, but may include: Spread rumors; damage property or belongings; undermine their success.

Vocabulary

1. coot
2. eons
3. gawked
4. confetti
5. opponent
6. testimony
7. incubating
8. pickpocket
9. distraction
10. hibernating

20

1.

a) F
b) T
c) T
d) F
e) T
f) F

2.

a) 5
b) 2
c) 6
d) 3
e) 1
f) 4

21

1.
Maniac has a happy life and does not seem to be aware of the racial issues or the trouble he may be causing.

2.
a) He doesn't like white people; doesn't want a white boy living in the neighborhood.
b) He kept repeating his address.

3.
The prize is pizza for one year and Maniac is allergic to pizza.

4.
Answers will vary.

22

1.

a) He will have a home; someone to care for him.

b) Help him with the chores and his job; keep him company.

Vocabulary

1. claptrap
2. dumbfounded
3. notion
4. zep
5. robust
6. rookies
7. recognition
8. sleazy
9. immortality
10. spree

1.

a) ✓ **C**
b) ✓ **B**
c) ✓ **D**
d) ✓ **A**
e) ✓ **D**
f) ✓ **C**

1.

Answers will vary, but may include: Raggy clothes, skinny, dirty, scratched skin, was unconscious.

2.

Answers will vary, but may include: Kind, cares about people; concerned about Maniac's safety; picks him up and carries him to the band shell; covers him with a jacket.

3.

Answers will vary.

Vocabulary

Across

2. languished
6. portable
7. traditional
8. preposterous
9. blarney
11. meandering
12. pommel
13. lavatory
14. filigreed

Down

1. mammoth
3. stoic
4. geezer
5. knack
6. pallbearers
10. repertoire

1.

a) F
b) T
c) T
d) F
e) T
f) T
g) F
h) F

2.

a) 6
b) 4
c) 2
d) 7
e) 3
f) 1
g) 5

1.

Maniac: 1. hugs Grayson; cooks for him; 2. won't give up trying to hit the stopball or trying to teach Grayson to read; 3. uses baseball talk to teach reading.

Grayson: 1. teaches Maniac some baseball tips; 2. gives Maniac his treasured baseball glove; 3. shares 101 Band Shell Boulevard with Maniac.

2.

a) Squeezed Grayson's hand; began talking to him; began to read aloud; lay down beside him; started to cry.

b) He cannot believe that Grayson is gone. He loved the old man; now he has no one.

3.

Answers will vary, but may include: He began to run and run so he could run away from the truth of the situation.

EZ✓

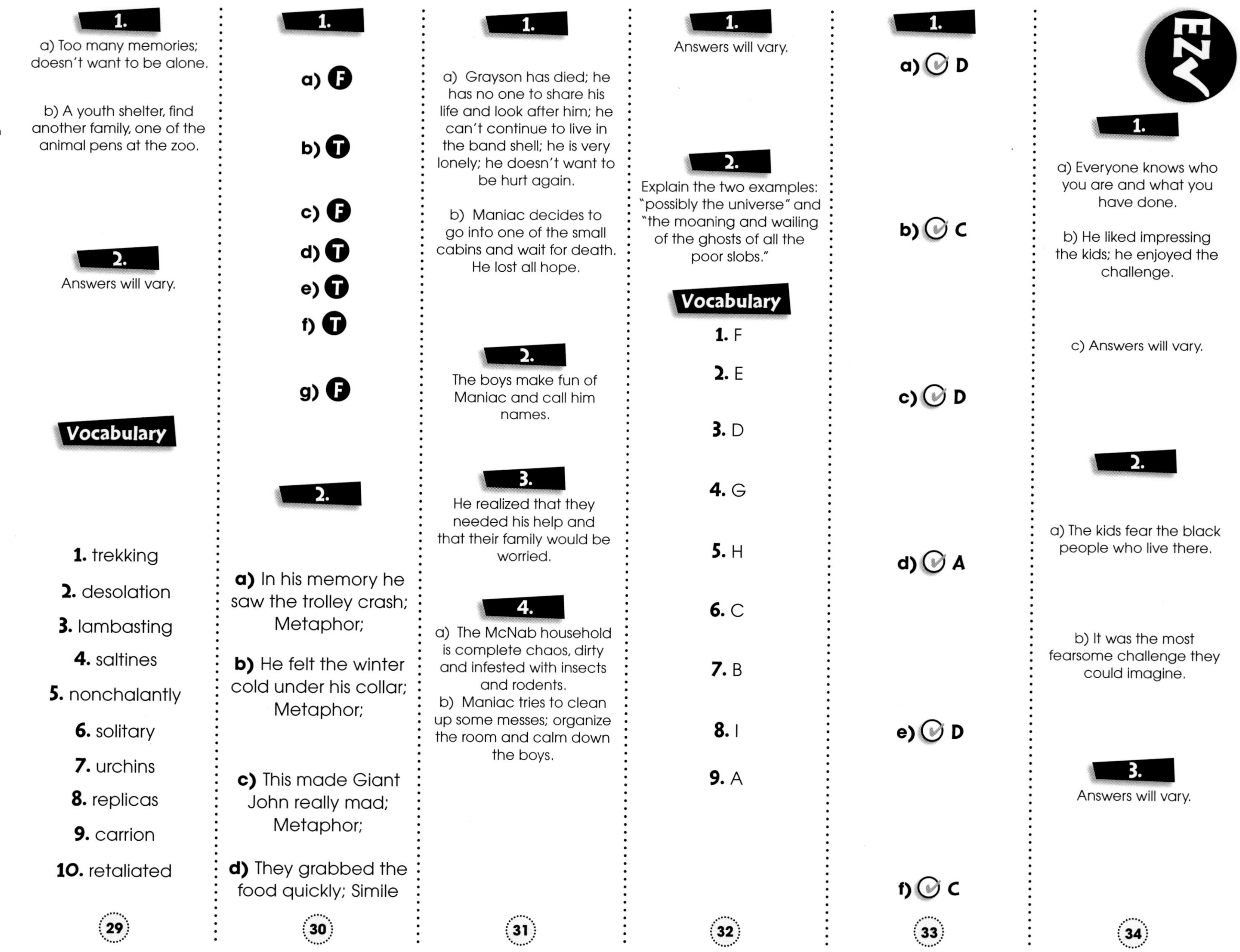

1.

a) Too many memories; doesn't want to be alone.

b) A youth shelter, find another family, one of the animal pens at the zoo.

2.

Answers will vary.

Vocabulary

1. trekking
2. desolation
3. lambasting
4. saltines
5. nonchalantly
6. solitary
7. urchins
8. replicas
9. carrion
10. retaliated

29

1.

a) F
b) T
c) F
d) T
e) T
f) T
g) F

2.

a) In his memory he saw the trolley crash; Metaphor;

b) He felt the winter cold under his collar; Metaphor;

c) This made Giant John really mad; Metaphor;

d) They grabbed the food quickly; Simile

30

1.

a) Grayson has died; he has no one to share his life and look after him; he can't continue to live in the band shell; he is very lonely; he doesn't want to be hurt again.

b) Maniac decides to go into one of the small cabins and wait for death. He lost all hope.

2.

The boys make fun of Maniac and call him names.

3.

He realized that they needed his help and that their family would be worried.

4.

a) The McNab household is complete chaos, dirty and infested with insects and rodents.
b) Maniac tries to clean up some messes; organize the room and calm down the boys.

31

1.

Answers will vary.

2.

Explain the two examples: "possibly the universe" and "the moaning and wailing of the ghosts of all the poor slobs."

Vocabulary

1. F
2. E
3. D
4. G
5. H
6. C
7. B
8. I
9. A

32

1.

a) D
b) C
c) D
d) A
e) D
f) C

33

1.

a) Everyone knows who you are and what you have done.

b) He liked impressing the kids; he enjoyed the challenge.

c) Answers will vary.

2.

a) The kids fear the black people who live there.

b) It was the most fearsome challenge they could imagine.

3.

Answers will vary.

34

35

1.

Answers will vary, but may include: walking, sleeping, reading, hobbies, "me" time.

Vocabulary

Sentences will vary.

36

1.

a) reacted to seeing a hero right here in their midst

b) got very angry, ranted

c) very angry, evil look on his face

d) he could feel the anger ripping through him

e) laughter stopped abruptly

2.

Answers will vary.

37

1.

a) Free pizza; organized a marble tournament on the schoolyard; read and took them to the library.

b) He has no place else to go; he thinks he can help the two younger boys to have a better life.

2.

Answers will vary, but may include: Mars Bar was tough and they might respect him.

3.

Illustrations will vary.

38

1.

Answers will vary.

2.

Answers will vary.

Vocabulary

a) constellations

b) slathered

c) veered

d) random

e) congregations

f) rasping

g) amplified

h) wrenching

i) trestle

j) dovetailed

39

1.

a) F

b) F

c) T

d) T

e) F

f) T

2.

a) 6

b) 3

c) 12

d) 1

e) 8

f) 10

g) 5

h) 11

i) 2

j) 7

k) 9

l) 4

40

1.

Answers will vary, but may include: He wanted to be friends with Maniac; get to know him.

2.

Answers will vary, but may include: screaming, wild-eyed, crying, soaking wet, feet slathered with coal-black mud, shrieked, babbled.

3.

Answers will vary, but may include: Maniac isn't afraid of anything; he always comes to the rescue; he has a connection to the McNab boys.

4.

Answers will vary, but may include: He needed to justify why he didn't rescue Russell.

5.

Answers will vary.

EZ✓

Word Search Puzzle

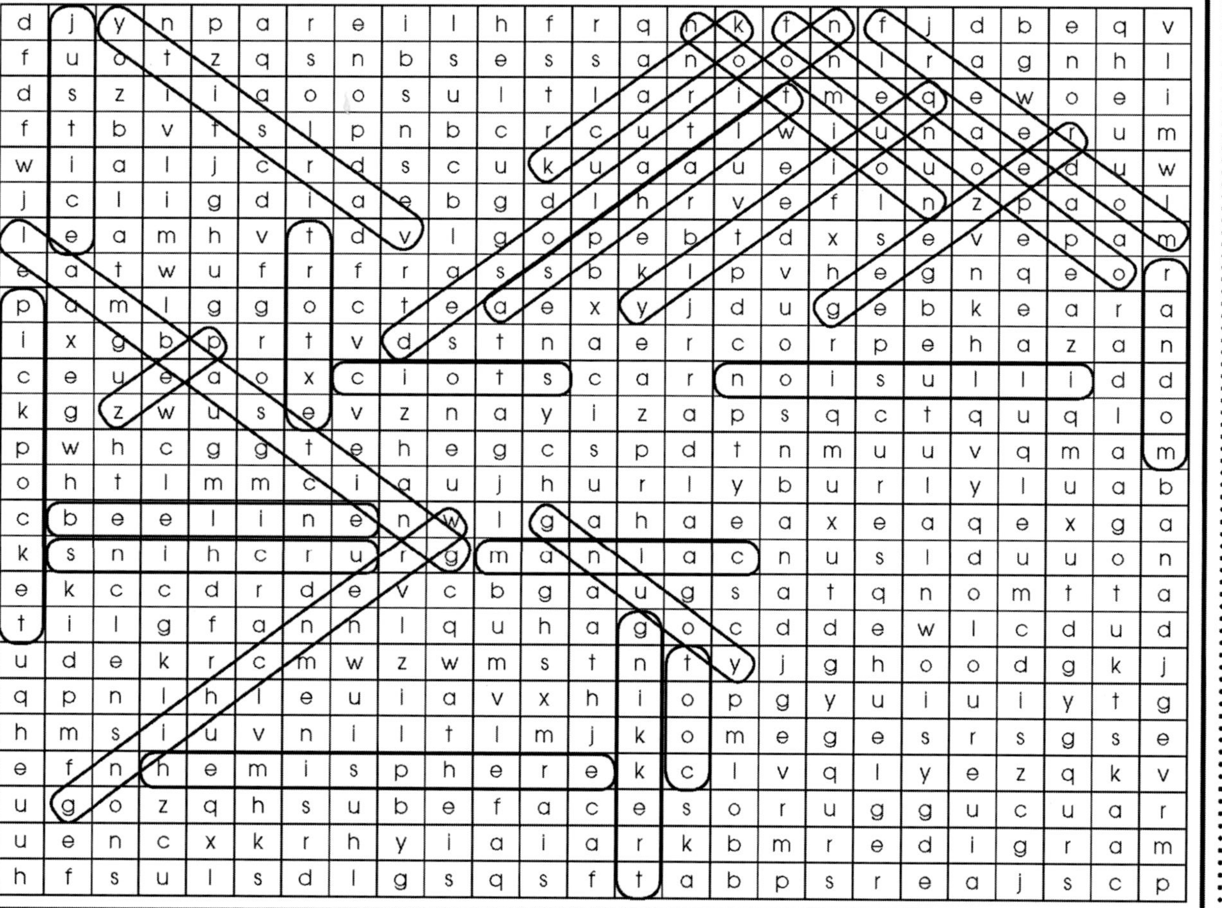

1.

He ran away because they didn't want him and he was very unhappy. He didn't really have a plan he just starting running and running.

2.

Mrs. Pickwell willingly fed any person who came to her house who was needy even though she was not a wealthy person.

3.

Jeffrey became Maniac Magee because of all of his daring feats: intercepting a football pass from a star player; rescuing a boy from Finsterwald's yard; hitting Giant John's fastball and the frog.

4.

Staying with the Beale family gave Maniac an address and a real family who cared for him.

5.

Maniac didn't see white people as all that different from blacks and couldn't figure out why the old man was so angry with him.

6.

The prize was pizza for a year and Maniac was allergic to pizza.

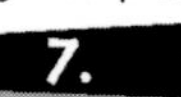

7.

Grayson was the father/ grandfather figure for Maniac. They both filled a need in each others' lives.

8.

Grayson wanted Maniac to teach him to read.

9.

He began to talk, to read aloud and then to cry. After the funeral, Maniac started running and running.

10.

Answers will vary.

11.

The McNab household was without rules or consideration for others. It was dirty and infested. Maniac stayed there because he didn't have anywhere else to go in winter.

12.

Maniac had a panic attack thinking about his parents' accident that took their lives.

13.

Answers will vary.

14.

Answers will vary.

44 45 46

Biography of Maniac Magee

Write a biography of Maniac Magee's life as it is told in this novel. Use the information in the sections to help you write your sentences. Try to highlight the most important events in Maniac's life.

Section 1 (CH. 1-5)	
Section 2 (CH. 6-10)	
Section 3 (CH. 11-14)	
Section 4 (CH. 15-21)	
Section 5 (CH. 22-25)	
Section 6 (CH. 26-32)	
Section 7 (CH. 33-35)	
Section 8 (CH. 36-39)	
Section 9 (CH. 40-43)	
Section 10 (CH. 44-46)	

New TV Show

Pretend that the story of Maniac Magee is going to be made into a miniseries for TV.

Your job is to create the first episode of the series.
Develop an outline by describing the setting, the characters, and the introduction to the plot.

Refer to Sections 1 and 2 for details if you need help.

Setting	Main Character	Minor Character

Minor Character
Introduction to Plot
Hints about future events

Now That's Funny!

There are many humorous situations in this novel. Select one situation to use to create a comic strip. Draw pictures to show the events of the situation in the order they happened. Use speech bubbles to record the dialogue between the characters.

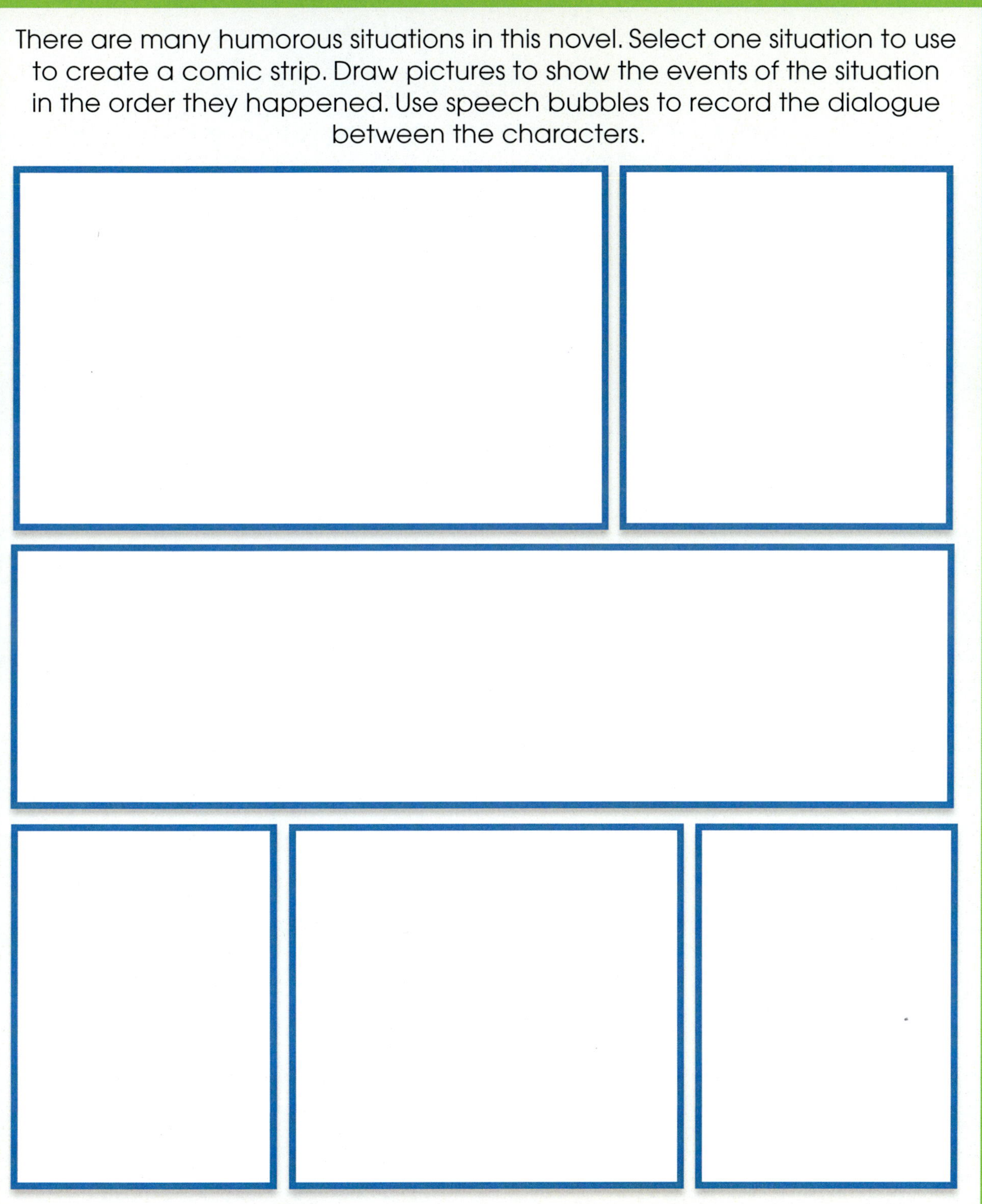

- **RSL.5.1** Quote accurately from a text when explaining what the text says explicitly and when drawing inferences from the text.
- **RSL.5.2** Determine a theme of a story, drama, or poem from details in the text, including how characters in a story or drama respond to challenges or how the speaker in a poem reflects upon a topic; summarize the text.
- **RSL.5.3** Compare and contrast two or more characters, settings, or events in a story or drama, drawing on specific details in the text.
- **RSL.5.4** Determine the meaning of words and phrases as they are used in a text, including figurative language such as metaphors and similes.
- **RSL.5.5** Explain how a series of chapters, scenes, or stanzas fits together to provide the overall structure of a particular story, drama, or poem.
- **RSL.5.6** Describe how a narrator's or speaker's point of view influences how events are described.
- **RSL.5.9** Compare and contrast stories in the same genre on their approaches to similar themes and topics.
- **RSL.5.10** By the end of the year read and comprehend literature, including stories, dramas, and poetry, at the high end of the grades 4–5 text complexity band independently and proficiently.
- **RSL.6.1** Cite textual evidence to support analysis of what the text says explicitly as well as inferences drawn from the text.
- **RSL.6.2** Determine a theme or central idea of a text and how it is conveyed through particular details; provide a summary of the text distinct from personal opinions or judgments.
- **RSL.6.3** Describe how a particular story's or drama's plot unfolds in a series of episodes as well as how the characters respond or change as the plot moves toward a resolution.
- **RSL.6.4** Determine the meaning of words and phrases as they are used in a text, including figurative and connotative meanings; analyze the impact of a specific word choice on meaning and tone.
- **RSL.6.5** Analyze how a particular sentence, chapter, scene, or stanza fits into the overall structure of a text and contributes to the development of the theme, setting, or plot.
- **RSL.6.6** Explain how an author develops the point of view of the narrator or speaker in a text.
- **RSL.6.10** By the end of the year read and comprehend literature, including stories, dramas, and poems, in the grades 6–8 text complexity band proficiently, with scaffolding as needed at the high end of the range.
- **RSFS.5.3** Know and apply grade-level phonics and word analysis skills in decoding words. **A)** Use combined knowledge of all letter-sound correspondences, syllabication patterns, and morphology to read accurately unfamiliar multisyllabic words in context and out of context.
- **RSFS.5.4** Read with sufficient accuracy and fluency to support comprehension. **A)** Read grade-level text with purpose and understanding. **B)** Read grade-level prose and poetry orally with accuracy, appropriate rate, and expression on successive readings. **C)** Use context to confirm or self-correct word recognition and understanding, rereading as necessary.
- **WS.5.1** Write opinion pieces on topics or texts, supporting a point of view with reasons and information. **A)** Introduce a topic or text clearly, state an opinion, and create an organizational structure in which ideas are logically grouped to support the writer's purpose. **B)** Provide logically ordered reasons that are supported by facts and details. **C)** Link opinion and reasons using words, phrases, and clauses. **D)** Provide a concluding statement or section related to the opinion presented.
- **WS.5.2** Write informative/explanatory texts to examine a topic and convey ideas and information clearly. **A)** Introduce a topic clearly, provide a general observation and focus, and group related information logically; include formatting, illustrations, and multimedia when useful to aiding comprehension. **B)** Develop the topic with facts, definitions, concrete details, quotations, or other information and examples related to the topic. **C)** Link ideas within and across categories of information using words, phrases, and clauses. **D)** Use precise language and domain-specific vocabulary to inform about or explain the topic. **E)** Provide a concluding statement or section related to the information or explanation presented.
- **WS.5.3** Write narratives to develop real or imagined experiences or events using effective technique, descriptive details, and clear event sequences. Orient the reader by establishing a situation and introducing a narrator and/or characters; organize an event sequence that unfolds naturally. **B)** Use narrative techniques, such as dialogue, description, and pacing, to develop experiences and events or show the responses of characters to situations. **C)** Use a variety of transitional words, phrases, and clauses to manage the sequence of events. **D)** Use concrete words and phrases and sensory details to convey experiences and events precisely. **E)** Provide a conclusion that follows from the narrated experiences or events.
- **WS.5.4** Produce clear and coherent writing in which the development and organization are appropriate to task, purpose, and audience.
- **WS.5.7** Conduct short research projects that use several sources to build knowledge through investigation of different aspects of a topic.
- **WS.5.8** Recall relevant information from experiences or gather relevant information from print and digital sources; summarize or paraphrase information in notes and finished work, and provide a list of sources.
- **WS.5.9** Recall relevant information from experiences or gather relevant information from print and digital sources; summarize or paraphrase information in notes and finished work, and provide a list of sources.
- **WS.6.1** Write arguments to support claims with clear reasons and relevant evidence. **A)** Introduce claim(s) and organize the reasons and evidence clearly. **B)** Support claim(s) with clear reasons and relevant evidence, using credible sources and demonstrating an understanding of the topic or text. **C)** Use words, phrases, and clauses to clarify the relationships among claim(s) and reasons. **D)** Establish and maintain a formal style. **E)** Provide a concluding statement or section that follows from the argument presented.
- **WS.6.2** Write informative/explanatory texts to examine a topic and convey ideas, concepts, and information through the selection, organization, and analysis of relevant content. **A)** Introduce a topic; organize ideas, concepts, and information, using strategies such as definition, classification, comparison/contrast, and cause/effect; include formatting, graphics, and multimedia when useful to aiding comprehension. **B)** Develop the topic with relevant facts, definitions, concrete details, quotations, or other information and examples. **C)** Use appropriate transitions to clarify the relationships among ideas and concepts. **D)** Use precise language and domain-specific vocabulary to inform about or explain the topic. **E)** Establish and maintain a formal style. **F)** Provide a concluding statement or section that follows from the information or explanation presented.
- **WS.6.3** Write narratives to develop real or imagined experiences or events using effective technique, relevant descriptive details, and well-structured event sequences. **A)** Engage and orient the reader by establishing a context and introducing a narrator and/or characters; organize an event sequence that unfolds naturally and logically. **B)** Use narrative techniques, such as dialogue, pacing, and description, to develop experiences, events, and/or characters. **C)** Use a variety of transition words, phrases, and clauses to convey sequence and signal shifts from one time frame or setting to another. **D)** Use precise words and phrases, relevant descriptive details, and sensory language to convey experiences and events. **E)** Provide a conclusion that follows from the narrated experiences or events.
- **WS.6.4** Produce clear and coherent writing in which the development, organization, and style are appropriate to task, purpose, and audience.
- **WS.6.7** Conduct short research projects to answer a question, drawing on several sources and refocusing the inquiry when appropriate.
- **WS.6.8** Gather relevant information from multiple print and digital sources; assess the credibility of each source; and quote or paraphrase the data and conclusions of others while avoiding plagiarism and providing basic bibliographic information for sources.
- **WS.6.9** Draw evidence from literary or informational texts to support analysis, reflection, and research. **A)** Apply *grade 6 Reading standards* to literature. **B)** Apply *grade 6 Reading standards* to literary nonfiction.